W9-BNL-428

EXTREME BIOLOGY

Survival of the Fittest

Extreme Adaptations

Louise Spilsbury

 Gareth Stevens
PUBLISHING

Please visit our website, **www.garethstevens.com**. For a free color catalog of all our high-quality books, call toll free 1-800-542-2595 or fax 1-877-542-2596.

Library of Congress Cataloging-in-Publication Data

Spilsbury, Louise, author.
 Survival of the fittest : extreme adaptations / Louise Spilsbury.
     pages cm. — (Extreme biology)
 Includes bibliographical references and index.
ISBN 978-1-4824-2252-8 (pbk.)
ISBN 978-1-4824-2253-5 (6 pack)
ISBN 978-1-4824-2250-4 (library binding)
1. Animal behavior—Juvenile literature. 2. Animals—Adaptation—Juvenile literature. 3. Adaptation (Biology)—Juvenile literature. I. Title.
 QL751.5.S675 2015
 591.5—dc23

                                2014027568

First Edition

Published in 2015 by
Gareth Stevens Publishing
111 East 14th Street, Suite 349
New York, NY 10003

© 2015 Gareth Stevens Publishing

Produced by: Calcium, www.calciumcreative.co.uk
Designed by: Paul Myerscough
Edited by: Sarah Eason and John Andrews
Picture research by: Rachel Blount

Photo credits: Cover: Shutterstock: J Reineke; Inside: Dreamstime: Allocricetulus 30, Daniel Bellhouse 19, Christian C. Berclaz 18, Bevanward 32, Dennis Donohue 27, Bonnie Fink 42, Jnjhuz 3, 40, Chris Kruger 11, Chris Moncrieff 23, Orchidart 20, Pamela Peters 4, Stephan Pietzko 41, Schnappschusshelge 15, Mogens Trolle 10, Twildlife 36, Nick Vermeulen 22; Shutterstock: Henk Bentlage 14, Mircea Bezergheanu 43, Nick Biemans 44, Ryan M. Bolton 5, Chantelle Bosch 33, Tony Brindley 25, Critterbiz 9, Curioso 17, Agustin Esmoris 29, Sergey Krasnoshchokov 24, D. Kucharski K. Kucharska 34, Petr Malyshev 38, Petrova Maria 39, Silviu Matei 37, Matteo Photos 21, MattiaATH 1, 16, Dave Montreuil 6, 7, Sari ONeal 13, Oksana2010 12, Pablo Mendez Rodriguez 35, Becky Sheridan 45, B G Smith 28, Gleb Tarro 26, John Tunney 8, Feng Yu 31.

All rights reserved. No part of this book may be reproduced in any form without permission from the publisher, except by reviewer.

Printed in the United States of America
CPSIA compliance information: Batch #CW15GS: For further information contact Gareth Stevens, New York, New York at 1-800-542-2595.

Contents

Chapter 1

Hunting Tactics

A lioness crouches behind the tall grass, her eyes fixed on the gazelle. Her powerful muscles are tensed, and her sharp teeth and claws are at the ready. If the attack fails, the lioness and her cubs will go hungry. If the gazelle fails to escape, by running fast and leaping high, it will die. They, like all animals, have special adaptations to help them succeed and survive.

Ways to Adapt

A lioness's fur is colored to camouflage her against the dry grasses where she lives. This is a physical adaptation. She often crouches low and sneaks up on prey before chasing it. This is a behavioral adaptation. Most animals use both types of adaptations to get shelter, escape danger, find mates, or locate food in the places where they live. In this book, we explore behavioral adaptations, and in this first chapter, we look at the hunting tactics animals use to catch food.

Lions are heavy and cannot run fast for long. So they stalk their prey before pouncing.

Alligator Snapping Turtle

The alligator snapping turtle is the largest freshwater turtle in North America. With its heavy, armored body, it weighs around 170 pounds (77 kg). This brute of a turtle is big and powerful but not fast enough to chase its fish prey. Instead, it lies patiently in wait in the murky waters where it lives with its jaws wide open, striking only when its prey comes close.

Extra Extreme

The alligator snapping turtle has a smart way to attract fish—a built-in lure. A pink piece of flesh sticks out from its tongue, looking a bit like a worm. When a fish swims in to investigate, the turtle snaps and grabs it.

Alligator snapping turtles have powerful jaws that can crunch through bone.

Black Heron

The black heron is sometimes called the umbrella bird because it stands in shallow water with its wings spread above its head like an umbrella. Why does it behave like this?

Stealthy Stabber

The black heron uses this umbrella as a stealth tactic so it can stab fish and then eat them. The umbrella shades the water, which reduces glare from sunlight overhead so the heron can see what is moving under the surface. The shade also attracts fish and amphibians hoping to hide in the darker waters. A black heron walks slowly around the marshy place where it lives and forms the umbrella for just a few seconds before moving on and repeating the behavior.

Without its umbrella, a black heron would find fewer prey.

Family Meals

Black herons nest together in groups, called colonies, with other types of herons. The male calls, stretches out his neck, and collects sticks to attract a female. If she wants to mate and breed with him, the two build a nest together in a tree above water and then raise up to four young. The parents regurgitate chewed up fish from their stomachs to their mouths to feed the young. The first hatchling gets more food than the others because it is the biggest and demands more from its parents. The last hatchling may die of starvation.

Herons have sharp, dagger-shaped beaks to pierce or grab prey, which they then usually swallow whole.

Extreme!

Tempting Toes

The black heron has some physical adaptations that help the umbrella stealth tactic work. Its especially broad wing feathers are shaped to link together and stop any sunlight from passing through them. The bird also has yellow feet that it shakes underwater, which attracts the attention of passing fish.

Humpback Whale

The 40-ton (36-mt) humpback whale has a problem. This giant of the ocean needs to eat around 3,000 pounds (1,360 kg) of food a day. However, by working in groups and using smart catching skills, the whales have found methods of filling up fast.

Food Filters

Humpbacks are baleen whales. Instead of teeth, they have long curtains of bristles, called baleen, in their jaws. They take a mouthful of water and use their giant tongues to push it back out through the baleen to trap any fish or krill, a kind of small shrimp, that the water contained. They then swallow the trapped food.

A humpback takes in huge mouthfuls of water. It cannot breathe through its mouth—it uses a blowhole on its head instead.

Humpbacks use "bubble nets" to drive fish up to the surface. The fish are trapped by the bubbles and cannot escape.

Amazing Air Net

When there is little prey in each mouthful of water, humpbacks need to spend far more time and energy feeding than when the water is more bountiful. To get bigger mouthfuls of food, groups, or pods, of humpbacks use "bubble nets." Whales find a school of fish and take turns diving up to 600 feet (180 m) to get underneath the school. They form a circle and blow air from the blowholes on their heads. The bubbles rise, forming a net of bubbles that traps the prey. Each whale then takes its turn swimming up inside the net to feast on the fish.

Extreme!

Mealtime Methods

Humpbacks are not the only sea mammals that hunt in pods. Sometimes killer whales, or orcas, make waves with their tails to wash resting seals off floating ice into the teeth of a waiting orca. Pods of their close relatives, dolphins, chase fish schools onto mud banks and lie in wait with mouths open as the panicking fish try to leap to safety.

Wild Dog

African wild dogs live in sociable packs of between 6 and 20 family members. When they hunt together, they can use their combined power to kill animals much larger than themselves. They favor antelopes but sometimes hunt zebras 10 times the weight of one dog.

Meat-Eating Marathon

At the start of a hunt, the wild dogs in a pack circulate and howl. The adult dogs walk and then run toward a herd of potential prey. One animal, identified as being weaker than the others, is targeted, and the pack may chase it for miles. Some dogs run near the prey and others lag behind, saving energy to take over once the leaders tire. At the end of this marathon, the pack sink their teeth into the exhausted prey.

By working as a team, wild dogs can chase off scavengers such as hyenas that may injure them while trying to steal their prey.

The African wild dog has excellent eyesight and big ears to listen to pack calls.

Dinnertime for Dogs

Pack leaders usually let weaker adults eat first while keeping watch for hyenas. The dogs eat what they can and then return to the rest of the pack, including females with very young pups and other adults that babysit older youngsters. These pack members whine and beg for food, and the hunters regurgitate meat from their stomachs for them to eat.

Extra Extreme

African wild dogs can run at speeds of up to 35 miles per hour (56 kph), faster than Olympic sprinter Usain Bolt. The dogs can also maintain the speed for several miles. A wild dog pack searches for food over a wide area, which can measure as much as 900 square miles (2,300 sq km). That is bigger than the combined areas of Chicago and Los Angeles.

Chapter 2

Keeping Safe

Animals that are hunted by other animals need ways to keep safe. Many animals have physical adaptations to protect them, like body colors or markings, called camouflage, that make them blend into the background of the habitat where they live. Animals have ways of behaving to protect themselves, too.

Take Cover!

Different species of animals have different behavioral adaptations that keep them safe. When a hedgehog is threatened, it rolls itself into a tight ball. The spikes over its back then protect its soft stomach and nose. Rabbits run into underground dens when they hear predators, and cats climb trees to escape when they are chased. Living in groups, or herds, also protects animals. Rain forest chimpanzees, for example, live together so they can warn each other if they spot danger.

Hedgehogs roll into balls to deter predators with their sharp spikes.

Playing Dead

When an opossum is frightened, it freezes with terror. It falls to the ground on its side, with its legs stretched out, goes totally limp, and stays still. When an animal runs, some predators get excited and want to attack. A motionless opossum does not excite their appetite, so they leave it in peace. Gradually the opossum comes around again and wanders off safely.

Extra Extreme

Opossums can even fake sickness to escape from predators. They build up a lot of spit, or saliva, that they drool from their mouths and even blow bubbles out of their noses. This makes it look as if they could be carrying a disease, so predators leave them alone.

Opossums may play dead for up to four hours!

Meerkat

Meerkats are small, furry animals that face constant danger because they have many predators. Birds of prey, such as eagles and hawks, hunt them from the air. Jackals, wild cats, and big snakes hunt them on the ground. To keep safe, meerkats have developed smart ways of behaving.

Guard Duty

Meerkats eat mostly insects, spiders, and scorpions that they dig from under the ground. So, when they feed, meerkats cannot watch for predators. That is why they live in groups of up to 30 animals, called mobs. While most meerkats are feeding, one or two others act as lookouts. They climb trees or mounds of earth and stand tall, propped up on their stiff tails, watching out for danger from the air and on the ground.

Guard duty lasts about an hour before another meerkat takes its turn watching for predators.

Warning Calls

If a guard spots a predator, it lets out a distinctive warning call. Instantly, all the meerkats race to the nearest entrance of their extensive underground tunnel network. If a predator is too close, meerkats dig quickly to create a cloud of dust in the hope that this will confuse the predator long enough to give them time to escape.

A meerkat has a keen sense of smell and sharp teeth to find and capture prey.

Extreme!

Sounds for Safety

Meerkats make different sounds to mean different things. A meerkat's warning call sounds like a shrill bark. Meerkat guards make a different sound to tell the mob when the coast is clear, and their calls get louder and faster as a predator gets closer and closer.

Zebra

Zebras live on open grasslands in Africa, where lions, hyenas, and other predators sneak up on these distinctively striped animals from behind the tall, dry grasses. To keep safe, zebras gather together in huge herds of hundreds or even thousands of animals.

Awake to Dangers

Zebras are grazing animals, so they feed with their heads down. They raise their heads often to look and sniff for danger. In a large herd, that means there are many animals on the lookout, making it less likely a predator will be able to take the herd by surprise. At night, a zebra sleeps standing up only for an hour or so at a time, and only when a few other grazing zebras are awake, so there is always someone keeping guard.

Each zebra's stripe pattern is unique, like a human's fingerprints.

Extreme!

Confuse the Captor

A zebra's stripes help keep it safe, too. When zebras in a herd run away, the stripes make it hard for a lion to tell where one zebra ends and another begins. The lion gets confused and cannot work out which way each zebra is moving. This makes it hard for the predator to target a single zebra.

On the Run

If a predator attacks, zebras run away fast in all directions. Some run in zigzag patterns to make it harder for attackers to catch them. Zebras will gather around a mother and baby from their herd to protect them from a pack of hyenas. They then kick out with their powerful back legs to get rid of the snarling predators.

A baby zebra can run from the time it is just one hour old.

Chapter 3
Smart Tricks

All animals need food to survive, and some have very smart ways of getting the food they need. Sea otters, for example, use stones as hammers to knock abalone shells off rocks and to crack the hard shells open, so they can eat the animals inside. Chimpanzees are even smarter. They have developed a number of ingenious tools to help them get their food and drink.

Super Sponges and Sticks

Thirsty chimps make sponges by chewing leaves into mush, and then dipping them into puddles of water. The sponges soak up the liquid, which the chimps then drink. Chimpanzees also use sticks and rocks to smash open tough fruits or hard nutshells. They then use smaller sticks to pick out the bits of nut left in the shell that they cannot reach easily with their teeth or fingers.

Chimpanzees are extremely smart and can come up with ways of behaving to get what they need.

Snacks on Sticks

Chimpanzees also turn sticks into food-finding devices. They pick up a twig, rip off its leaves, break it to the right length, and bite it into the right shape. Then they dip the stick into a termite or ant nest to fish for food, wiping the insects into their mouths. Chimps use stick tools as well to scoop honey from bees' nests to avoid getting stung.

Chimpanzees shape and break sticks to make tools for finding food.

Extra Extreme

Crows know some smart tricks, too. They drop stones into water containers to raise the level of the liquid inside, so they can reach and drink it. Carrion crows drop walnuts onto crosswalks, so cars drive over the shells and break open the nuts. The birds wait until it is safe to cross before collecting their dinner.

Trap-Door Spider

Ambush attacks are the specialty of the trap-door spider. Rather than hunting down prey, this cunning creature makes a trap and lies in wait for its dinner to be delivered.

Setting the Trap

To make its trap, the trap-door spider digs out an underground tunnel or burrow using fang-like mouthparts. Its jaws move up and down and are full of tiny spikes that help the spider dig. Once the spider has dug a tunnel, it builds a door for the top from silk and earth. The trap-door is hinged on one side with silk, so it opens and closes easily. The spider covers the door with bits of leaf, twig, and rock to camouflage it.

The entrance to a spider's trap is almost impossible to spot unless the door is open.

Trap-door spiders use their burrows to ambush prey, hide from predators, and raise young.

Ambush!

When an unsuspecting insect—or even a frog, mouse, baby bird, or small snake—passes by, the spider feels the vibrations its movements make on the ground above. Then as quick as a flash, the spider throws open the trap-door and grabs the prey in its powerful jaws. It pulls its victim back down into the burrow and stabs downward with its sharp fangs to kill the prey.

Extreme!

Spider Nursery

Trap-door spiders have their young in burrows. A female lays her eggs there and covers them with silk to attach them to the burrow wall. She stays with the eggs until they hatch and then protects and feeds the young spiders. When they are about eight months old, the youngsters are ready to dig their own burrows and make their own traps.

Leafcutter Ant

Leafcutter ants are simply amazing. They are the farmers of the insect world, creating fertile underground backyards that supply their huge colonies with food.

Foliage Farming

Colonies of leafcutter ants in Central and South America may contain millions of individuals. To provide food for this huge number of hungry mouths, thousands of ants march out from their nest to collect leaves. They use their jaws to cut off pieces of leaf and carry these back. Deep inside the nest, ants chew the leaves into a pulp and release substances that encourage fungi to grow on it. Other ants tend the fungi garden, making sure it stays clean and grows well. Then the ants eat the fungi and feed it to the young larvae in the nest.

Leafcutter ants have powerful jaws that vibrate 1,000 times per second to clip off pieces of leaf.

Extra Extreme

Each tiny leafcutter ant can carry a load more than 50 times its own body weight. The amount of leaves cut from rain forests by these tough insect weight lifters adds up to about 15 percent of all the leaves that rain forests produce.

Jobs for All

The secret of the leafcutter ant colony's farming success is teamwork. Different ants in the colony do different jobs. Soldier ants defend the colony with their huge jaws. Worker ants collect the leaves, tend the gardens, and feed and care for the larvae. There are also some ants that release a substance that acts as a pesticide to kill off a particular mold that can damage the fungus. And there is even a group of tiny worker ants that ride on the backs of the leaf collectors to defend them from attack by predator flies.

To find the right kind of leaf, a leafcutter ant may travel hundreds of feet—a long way for an ant.

Chapter 4

Surviving Winter

When the weather gets cold, we put on sweaters and coats and turn up the heat to keep warm. Animals behave in a number of different ways to stay warm and survive the challenges of the extreme cold and lack of food they face in winter.

Caribou Migration

When winter comes, some animals move to warmer places to avoid the cold and to find food. This behavioral adaptation is called migration. Caribou are large deer that migrate every year between forests and tundras, in huge herds of up to half a million animals. The round trip can be as long as 3,000 miles (4,800 km). The tundra is very cold, harsh, and windy during the winter, so caribou migrate to forests farther south, where the weather is milder and there is more food.

Caribou have hooves that can spread out on snow or soft ground to stop them from sinking.

Seasonal Foods

Caribou herds split up in winter, and the animals spend their time feeding in forests. During the winter, they eat mainly lichens called reindeer moss, which they reach by digging under the snow. In spring, the caribou gather together in enormous herds to migrate north to the tundra. Throughout the summer, they eat grass, leaves, and buds. In the fall, they gather together again to migrate back to the forests.

Extra Extreme

The Arctic tern makes an incredible return trip of around 44,000 miles (71,000 km) between the North and South Poles each year. The seabird flies between breeding grounds in Greenland in the Arctic and the Weddell Sea on the shores of Antarctica. By the end of its lifetime, one of these far-flying birds has traveled the equivalent of three round trips to the moon.

Arctic terns catch fish such as sand eels for themselves and for their chicks to eat, and to fuel a monumental migration.

Grizzly Bear

Grizzly bears are huge animals anyway, but during the late summer and the fall, they gain even more weight. Grizzlies eat as much as they can and pile on the pounds because they need to build up large amounts of body fat. This allows them to survive in their dens during their winter sleep, called hibernation.

Digging a Den

Grizzly bears live in the mountains of North America, where winters are cold and the berries, plant roots, and small animals that these bears eat are scarce. So they find or make large, safe dens to rest in until spring when food is plentiful again. A den can be a rock cave, tree hollow, or a hole in a hillside or under tree roots.

Grizzlies stand in rivers to catch salmon migrating inland from the sea. Eating oily salmon helps fatten up bears quickly.

Large adult grizzly bears can be about 8 feet (2.5 m) long and weigh around 900 pounds (400 kg).

Deep Sleep

During its winter hibernation, a grizzly bear's heart rate slows down, its temperature drops, and it goes to sleep. To stay alive, the bear's body breaks down the fat stored up in summer and fall to use as food. By the time bears leave their dens in spring, they are very hungry and have usually lost up to one-third of their body weight. Mother bears are especially hungry and thin because they have been feeding babies in the den, too.

Extreme!

Smart Cubs

Amazingly, grizzly bear cubs are born while their mothers are asleep in their winter dens. Females usually give birth to twins, and after birth the two cubs crawl to their mother's belly to snuggle into her fur for warmth and feed on her milk, called suckling. The mother stays asleep while the cubs feed and grow, getting ready to follow their mother outside the den when spring comes.

Pika

Animals that live in places where summer growing seasons are short and winters are long often store food. They collect and stash it somewhere safe to eat during the barren winter when resources are low. The pikas of western North America are small, furry mammals that live in the mountains and spend a lot of their time foraging for food.

Building Food Supplies

Pikas scurry about rocky hillsides during the daytime gathering green plants like grasses, weeds, and tall wildflowers that are plentiful in spring and summer. They eat some and make piles of extra food that they lay out in the sun. The sun's heat dries the plants, which stops them from going moldy. Then the pikas carry the food into their dens in the rocks and store it until winter.

Pikas gather food in summer, when a lot of grasses and flowers grow in the mountains.

Winter Wanderings

Pika fur gets thicker in winter to help keep in the warmth, but pikas still spend most of the winter inside their dens to avoid the freezing cold and the biting winds. They eat the dried grasses they have stored to survive and only venture out to forage when the weather is good or if their food supply runs low. Then the pikas gather foods such as lichen and cushion plants, which still grow in winter.

Extreme!

Nut Knowledge

Squirrels in North America sort the acorns that they collect for winter before hiding them in the ground or in the hollows of trees. Acorns of red oak trees taste a little bitter but keep well, so squirrels tend to store these. It is the tastier nuts from white oak trees that are eaten first.

Squirrels collect and hide hundreds of acorns in underground stores. They remember where the stores are and defend them from other squirrels.

Chapter 5

Escaping the Heat

Animals can become weak and sick, and even die, if they get too hot and do not have enough water to drink. Some animals have to take drastic measures to stay cool and survive the extremes of very hot, dry climates.

Cool Behavior

Some animals use the heat to cool themselves. Kangaroos lick their forearms, so hot air evaporates the spit and takes some heat from the blood under their skin. Other animals go to extreme lengths to conserve water. Kangaroo rats, for example, produce bone-dry feces and only a tiny amount of highly concentrated urine. Many animals just get out of the way in the hottest times. Some, such as the little hopping jerboa that lives in deserts, are nocturnal, meaning they are only active at night, when temperatures are cooler.

The jerboa's long tail stops it from toppling over as it hops. It moves in zigzags and can leap high—useful skills for escaping from a predator.

A female burrowing owl has up to 12 young at a time that live in the safety of the burrow she digs.

Burrowing Owl

Unlike most owls, tiny burrowing owls live on the ground, some of the time in burrows. Staying underground in the hottest part of the day stops them from getting too hot and keeps them safe from predators such as hawks. Burrows are also safe places to rear young owls. Burrowing owls may dig their own nests, but quite often they save their energy by taking over a hole left by a prairie dog or armadillo.

Extra Extreme

It might sound disgusting, but a burrowing owl collects and smears mammal poop around its burrow entrance. This attracts dung beetles, which are one of the owl's favorite snacks. There are also many other things on an owl's menu, from lizards and scorpions, to doves and mice.

Sidewinder Snake

In the deserts of the United States and Africa, j-shaped marks left in the sand give a clue as to how sidewinder snakes deal with their extreme environment. It is all about keeping their bodies off the baking-hot sand.

Desert Dances

Sidewinders live in deserts where daytime temperatures are usually above 104°F (40°C). To avoid dragging the whole of their bellies—which are up to 2.5 feet (76 cm) long—over the burning-hot sand, the snakes loop and raise their bodies into waves so that just two short sections of it touch the sand at any time. They then push against these points to move sideways. When not moving, the snakes quickly burrow down under the desert surface to cooler sand or dive into the nearest animal burrow for shade.

The sidewinder's special way of moving leaves curvy marks in the sand.

Sidewinders are pink, orange, gray, or tan with dark spots, which makes them tricky to spot in their sandy habitats.

Heat Seeker

At night, desert temperatures plummet and sidewinders go hunting on the cooling sand. They use special pits between their eyes and nostrils to sense heat given off by their favorite prey—rodents. Sidewinders approach silently in the dark and in the blink of an eye their large, curved fangs flick forward and jab into their prey. The fangs inject venom, a kind of poison, from glands in the snakes' heads. This stops prey from moving, so the snakes can stretch their jaws wide and swallow it whole.

Extreme!

Reptile Rattle

A sidewinder has a built-in sound effect to scare off predators such as hawks and owls. The rattle at the end of its tail makes a hiss or buzz that tells predators it is a poisonous snake. The rattle is made from rings of keratin—the same material that our fingernails are made from—that scrape together when shaken.

Spadefoot Toad

The spadefoot toad is a golf-ball-sized amphibian that remains buried under hot desert sand for months until the first signs of rain. Then it emerges, breeds, feeds, and buries itself before the soil dries up again.

Rain Alert

Spadefoot toads spend most of the year in a trance in underground burrows. This slow-motion existence, where the toads neither feed nor drink, is called estivation. Yet they still listen for the falling raindrops or vibrations of thunder that mark the start of the rainy season. Then the toads wake and burrow upward. The males start to bleat to attract females to mate, and the females lay hundreds of eggs in temporary ponds formed when it rains.

Rain is heavy and infrequent where spadefoots live. So they need to dig to the surface fast while the ground is soft.

Extra Extreme

Hurried Meals

Once spadefoot polliwogs hatch after it rains, they need to get enough food to change into toadlets before the pools they live in dry up. The polliwogs graze on moss, water fleas, and anything else they can find. Toadlets and adults hop around to also find food in a hurry. They flick out their tongues to catch termites, grasshoppers, and spiders. Some eat all they need to survive estivation in just one sitting. The toads then take a big drink and burrow downward once more.

When temperatures are very high and pools are drying up fast, some spadefoot polliwogs become cannibals. They develop oversized heads, strong jaw muscles, and beak-shaped mouths to eat smaller tadpoles. However, cannibal polliwogs do have some table manners—if other toad species are in their pool, they eat them first.

Spadefoot toads are named for the horny, spade-shaped growths on their back feet that they use for digging.

Jackrabbit

Jackrabbits are large hares with enormous ears and hind feet. These features help them cope with the heat of the day and listen for predators. However, their ability to survive relies on being most active under the cover of darkness.

Nighttime Nibbler

Jackrabbits are active after dusk, when the temperature drops in the dry shrublands of North America they inhabit. They see well at night and their giant ears hear even the quietest rustle that could signal danger. Jackrabbits use their heavy-duty front teeth to graze on anything from grasses to twigs. The plants are also their source of water. By day, jackrabbits snooze or lie still, crouched flat in shady hollows under bushes.

Having eyes on the sides of its head allows a jackrabbit to see all around it and spot danger from every direction.

Jackrabbits hop along on their 1-foot (30.5-cm) long hind feet quicker than the fastest human sprinter can run.

Around-the-Clock Dangers

If a jackrabbit makes a wrong move during the day, a jackal, eagle, or hawk could pounce. At night, owls are the main danger. To survive, jackrabbits flee fast, their hind legs pushing them along with powerful hops. They can leap more than 10 feet (3 m) high and cover the ground at up to 40 miles per hour (64 kph). However, it is not all about speed. Jackrabbits also run in zigzags and alternately put up one ear and then the other to flash a black-and-white pattern. These behaviors can confuse their pursuers.

Extreme!

Helpful Heartbeat

When jackrabbits are hidden but know predators are close by, they can slow their heartbeats so their breathing cannot be heard. An instant before they start running for their lives, their heart rates shoot up three times faster than normal and they are ready to take evasive action.

Chapter 6
Making Shelters

Animals need shelters to keep them dry and warm in cold places, and cool and protected from sunlight in hot ones. An animal's shelter is also a place where it can hide from predators and have babies safely. Different animals have different ways of making their homes.

Do-It-Yourself Homes

Some animals have great building skills. Birds make nests from mud, feathers, and plant materials to keep eggs and nestlings safe. Like birds, squirrels build large nests in trees out of leaves and twigs. Other animals simply make use of what is lying around them. The hermit crab is born without a shell, so it finds an empty shell to live in. When it grows too big for one shell, the crab moves to a bigger one.

Unless a hermit crab finds a shell that is the right size to live in, its soft body is open to attack by predators.

Animal Weavers

Weaverbirds make the most extreme nests of all—beautiful and elaborate structures created by the careful looping and weaving of strands of grass or strips of leaves. A male weaverbird weaves the nest in the shape of an upside-down bottle, with a narrow, downward-facing entrance at the bottom so predators find it hard to get in. When a male is happy with his handiwork, he hangs upside down from it while calling out and gently flapping his wings to attract a female.

Sociable weaver nests are so well built that they can last for 100 years!

Extra Extreme

Sociable weavers go a step further and weave one gigantic nest for all the birds in their colony. This is the bird equivalent of a high-rise apartment building. Groups of birds use twigs, grass, and straw to make lots of rooms and many entrances inside the nest until it is so big that up to 100 families can live inside.

Beaver Lodge

Beavers are the most famous builders of the animal world. These big rodents, each weighing around 60 pounds (27 kg), chop down trees and branches to construct giant homes, called lodges.

Chisel Mouth

Beaver teeth are like two pairs of giant chisels. Beavers use them to strip bark and leaves from trees for food, and to cut down trees for lodge construction. Beavers drag some tree branches underwater and anchor them there. The branches serve as an emergency food supply in case the pond freezes over in the winter and the beavers cannot get to fresh trees.

A beaver can bite through a 5-inch (13-cm) thick aspen tree in 3 minutes!

Extreme!

Talented Tail

Beavers have very wide tails. These are useful rudders when the rodents swim, and can be used to slap the water surface to warn others about approaching predators. On land, beavers use their tails to prop themselves up while they gnaw on trees. In the fall, a beaver's tail fattens up and is a useful source of food energy over the winter.

Beavers need good swimming skills to construct lodges like these and to swim in and out of them.

Lodges and Dams

Beavers build new lodges in the fall. They gnaw on small trees to cut them down and use their mouths to drag the branches into messy cone shapes. The lodges extend from lakes or pond banks into deeper waters, where the underwater entrances are located. The lodges have hollow centers lined with grass and mud. The lodges are where the beavers go to avoid predators such as wolves, to keep warm, and to raise young. When beavers live by rivers, they may construct branch-and-mud dams to block the flow of water and create lakes where they can more easily make lodges.

Prairie Dog Burrow

As their name suggests, prairie dogs live on prairies in the United States, Canada, and Mexico. Prairies are open areas of grassland with few trees or bushes for animals to shelter in, so prairie dogs work together to build incredible complexes of underground tunnels. These spread so far that they are known as "towns."

Building a Community

Prairie dogs live together in groups, called colonies, which number hundreds or even several thousands of animals. A town complex is made up of separate smaller areas in which different groups of prairie dogs live. Members of the colony all use their sharp, thick, black claws to help dig the burrows for their neighborhood. Each burrow consists of tunnels that lead to underground chambers or rooms and has at least two entrances or exits.

Prairie dogs collect grass to line the nurseries and sleeping chambers inside their burrows.

Inside a Burrow

Prairie dogs build the underground chambers for different purposes. They can rush into chambers near the surface to escape from predators. There are special toilet chambers where they deposit all their waste. Chambers deep below ground are for resting or sleeping, and some are lined with grass and used as nurseries, where baby prairie dogs are born and cared for.

Extreme!

Loud Lookout

When prairie dogs leave their burrows to feed, one stays on top of the burrow mound to act as a lookout. If it spots a predator, it barks a warning to the others. Prairie dogs have developed different sounds to mean different animals, such as "hawk" and "coyote." When the warning is sounded, prairie dogs run as fast as they can into the nearest burrow entrance hole.

Prairie dogs stand up on their back legs and open their mouths wide to warn other prairie dogs of any potential danger.

Chapter 7

Vital Behaviors

We have seen how making complex burrows, playing dead, living in huge herds, and many other extreme types of behavior can help animals survive. Behavioral adaptations can be inherited or learned from parents, who pass them on to offspring, generation after generation.

Time for School

Most young animals follow and watch their parents, and then through trial and error figure out how to do things for themselves—and survive. This is how young chimps learn to fish for ants and how young prairie dogs come to understand the warning signals that make their parents run for cover. Some animals, such as the raccoon, find new ways to adapt by themselves.

Many animals learn behaviors from their parents that help them survive.

Extra Extreme

Raccoon Raiders

The raccoon is a great example of behavioral adaptation in action. As people have destroyed its habitat, this mammal has changed its diet and the places where it lives in order to survive. The natural habitat for raccoons is the forest, where they nest in trees and search for foods such as berries by day and fish at night. However, as people have cut down more and more forests, raccoons have adapted their behavior. Today, many raccoons nest in attics, basements, garages, and sheds, instead of trees. Rather than forest foods, they eat leftovers found in the trash. Like all great survivors, they have adapted to changes in their environment to ensure their species continues to thrive.

Some animals, such as raccoons, rats, and foxes, can adapt their behaviors quickly, which is why they are so successful. As people change the environment by cutting down trees or building on grasslands, animals that cannot adapt die out. Some scientists think that up to three of the planet's species die out every hour because of problems like habitat destruction and pollution.

Raccoons are very successful at adapting to a variety of places and challenges, even reaching and raiding bird feeders!

Glossary

adaptations changes in an animal that help it stay alive

amphibians animals that live on land and in water, such as frogs

behavioral adaptation a way of acting or behaving that helps a living thing survive

blowhole a breathing hole on the top of a marine animal's head

breed to reproduce or have young

camouflage color or pattern that matches the surroundings and helps hide something

colony a group of plants or animals growing or living in the same place

estivation to spend a hot, dry season in a sleeplike state

evaporate to change from a liquid into a gas

feces the solid waste that leaves an animal's body

fungi (singular is fungus) a group of organisms that includes yeasts, mushrooms, and molds

herd a group of animals that live and move along together

hibernation the sleeplike state in which some animals spend winter

larvae (singular is larva) young animals, particularly insects, with different forms than adults

mammals warm-blooded animals that have hair or fur and feed milk to their young

migration the movement from one place to another

nocturnal active at night

pesticide a substance that kills insects

physical adaptation a body part that helps an animal survive

pollution substances that poison or contaminate air, land, or water

prairie an extensive, flat land that is covered mostly in grasses

predator an animal that kills other animals for food

prey an animal that is hunted by another animal for food

regurgitate to bring swallowed food up to the mouth again

rodents a group of small mammals, such as rats, that have strong gnawing teeth

scavengers animals that find and feed on dead animals or waste

school a large group of fish swimming together

species a type of living thing

suckling drinking milk from a female mammal's body

termite a small, pale, soft insect that lives in large colonies

tundra Arctic land where the ground is always frozen

venom poison produced by animals

For More Information

Books

Lew, Kristi. *Evolution: The Adaptation and Survival of Species* (Understanding Genetics). New York, NY: Rosen Publishing Group, 2010.

Sneddon, Robert. *Adaptation and Survival* (The Web of Life). North Mankato, MN: Raintree Freestyle, 2012.

Waldron, Melanie. *Adaptation* (Essential Life Science). North Mankato, MN: Heinemann InfoSearch, 2013.

Websites

Read more about adaptation at:
education.nationalgeographic.com/education/encyclopedia/adaptation/?ar_a=1

There are videos, facts, and more about animal adaptations at:
www.bbc.co.uk/nature/adaptations

See some interesting examples of adaptation at:
www.tburg.k12.ny.us/mcdonald/ANIMAL%20ADAPTATIONS/AAdapt.htm

Explore Antarctic animal adaptations at:
www.coolantarctica.com/Antarctica%20fact%20file/wildlife/antarctic_animal_adaptations.htm

Publisher's note to educators and parents: Our editors have carefully reviewed these websites to ensure that they are suitable for students. Many websites change frequently, however, and we cannot guarantee that a site's future contents will continue to meet our high standards of quality and educational value. Be advised that students should be closely supervised whenever they access the Internet.

Index